Table of Contents

Printed in the United States of America

First Printing, 2019

ISBN 9781797562360

www.tvmallory.com

VictoriaMallory@icloud.com

DAY 1

APPRECIATION

Being a mom is one of the greatest miracles of life. Psalm 127:3 says, "Children are a gift from the Lord..." When we begin to view them as a gift, we gather an appreciation to God for them. We cherish them, take care of them, nurture them and look after them; just as one treats any other special gift.

Whenever my kids are cutting up and acting all levels of cray cray, it's hard for me to view them as the precious gifts that they are. When there has been a mural painted with poop on the wall by an artistic toddler or a perfectly placed leggo under your foot at 3am while trying to relieve yourself it is a true challenge to remember that these rugrats are gifts that God so graciously gave us; not because we were so good, but simply because He is good! When my vision is clouded of this truth due to my children's disobedience, and/or their inability to comprehend what is seemingly common sense, it is in these moments that I'm reminded of women like Hannah and Rachel who dealt with fertility sensitivities. In their desperation, they wept bitterly and cried out to the one and only God who could not only fix the root of the issue but also open their womb and give them the ability to reproduce! (1 Samuel 1:9-28 & Genesis 30:1; 30:22-24).

I too have had my share of heartache by suffering three miscarriages (one nearly costing me my very life). I too understand the bitter taste of the pain associated with grave loss. I'm so appreciative that God is no respecter of persons, and therefore, what He has done for one, He is able and willing to do for anyone who believes!

These women were great examples of faith in my life pertaining to my fertility and beliefs. I realized that the more they (we) placed (place) their (our) trust in the One who could (can) change their (our) outcome and focused (focus) less on their (our) husband's inability to give them (us) what their (our) hearts desired (desire), their outcome changed and so did mine (and so can yours)!

4

Today is a great day to shift our perspective to that of appreciation of God's "leggo losing" gifts and ask Him how we can be a better steward with such individually wrapped special gifts. By shifting our perspective, we can view the poopy paintings as works of art.

Recite this prayer:

Dear God,

I ask for the patience to understand my special gifts. Grant me grace needed to love, care, protect and rear them according to Your will Father. I ask for Your forgiveness for my shortcomings and the times I've allowed stress to cloud my vision. Thank you for a new day and a new chance to get it "right."

In Jesus name, Amen.

SPILL YOUR HEART

DAY 2

APPRECIATION

Appreciation simply means the recognition and enjoyment of the good qualities of someone or something. When was the last time you showed yourself some appreciation? When was the last time you took yourself on a spa date or set a hair appointment? Can't recall? Neither can I! I say this jokingly, however, the truth still remains that I too allow the business of life to get in the way of making myself a priority. Some may think these things are superficial or lack importance, but I would like to challenge that thought. Pampering yourself, non-excessively of course, is not only healthy, but I dare say it is also mandatory! No one works a 9 to 5 corporate job without benefiting from their labor! Any work that goes without reward is slavery. God did not give us "gifts" to enslave us to them. It is quite the contrary! God has graced us with the task and ability to raise the next generation of Holy Spirit filled, selfless, devout believers, who are unashamed of the gospel of Christ. With such a task, we should occasionally reset, and by reset, I mean rest and recharge.

We rest by following Jesus' example. Jesus often withdrew to lonely places and prayed (Luke 5:16). I believe that there is a blessing in solitude. It is the place where we can cast all our cares on the Father through prayer and be regenerated in order to excel at the task given to us as mothers. Make it a point to find a quiet place to pray and just breathe. It is vital to your sanity as a mother!

Recharging is just as blissful as resting but a lot more fun! We recharge by recreation! Do the things that are exciting to you! Do activities that RE-CREATE energy and help your passions resurface! For me, it's watching a full season of House Wives of any county, or it's designing clothes. I really love making vlogs and looking through old footage or weirdly enough, watching chiropractor youtube videos, (don't ask). Even considering all those, there is nothing like dancing! It's like I was born to do it! When I'm recharging like this, it revs up a generator in me that can tackle anything, and the fire lasts long after I have left the studio and have come out of the shower. I am simply in a great mood and can approach obstacles with a clear mind.

Make today unusual by making it about you! Don't walk into day three of this devotional without showing yourself the tender loving care that you have earned. Show yourself the appreciation I'm sure your family has for you. Proverbs 31:31 says, "Honor her for all that her hands have done, and let her works bring her praise."

Recite this prayer:

Father God,

I thank you for entrusting me with such a mandate of raising the next generation of believers. I'm so grateful You have chosen me to contribute in such a great way! Father rid me of the guilt associated with pampering myself and bring people into my life that can be trusted with temporarily caring for the amazing gifts (children) you have given me while I reset. Last but certainly not least, guide my feet to the best and most affordable pedicurist in town!

In Jesus name, Amen.

SPILL YOUR HEART

_____

_____

_____

_____

_____

_____

_____

_____

_____

_____

_____

_____

_____

_____

_____

_____

_____

_____

DAY 3

APPRECIATION

A lot of us have heard the expression, "It takes a village to raise a child." The basic meaning, from my own perspective, is that child upbringing is a communal effort. This does not mean an entire village is held responsible for raising one's child, however, it does take a community of different people interacting with each other for children to grow and mature in diversity. I do believe that surrounding your children with a healthy community of believers from all walks of life not only offers your children culture but helps broaden their perspective on life in general.

It is important to understand that just as there are parental control options on TV programs, gaming systems, and internet websites, as a parent, you reserve the right to select and control who gets the opportunity to be a part of your children's "village." It is our responsibility as mommies to filter what our children are exposed to and to whom they are exposed to.

Who is a part of your village? Do your children have a healthy community? When was the last time you showed your children's grandparents, baby sitter/nanny, childcare provider, teacher, school bus driver, Pastor, cafeteria worker, crossing guard, relatives, friends or anyone who extends help that offers you a small break, here and there, some appreciation? Some of you are teachers and leaders and know exactly what I mean from both a mommy and a professional perspective. It's these seemingly small roles and contributions that bring the most benefit to us and our children's lives and it is your gentle acts of kindness and appreciation that really improve the quality of those benefits and sets the temperature of favor extended to your child(ren). The deciding factor that determines whether your child is looked at as another number in someone's profession or as a life someone feels privileged to have a small part in is directly connected to your open appreciation for your village.

Recite this Prayer:

Dear God,

Help me to never take for granted the amazing community you have placed around me. Help me to make it a priority to take time and show open appreciation for the people who are most instrumental to both mine and my kid(s) life. I thank you for my village God, and I pray a blessing over every person and their households that are a part of it. I ask You Lord that they receive the same love, patience, care, dedication, and time that they invest in my children back in multiple measures.

In Jesus name, Amen.

SPILL YOUR HEART

DAY 4

APPRECIATION

Now that we understand that children are gifts from God (Psalm 127:3) and appreciation is the recognition and enjoyment of the good qualities of someone or something, then we must recognize and/or acknowledge the Giver of said gifts. So often, we get consumed with the "business" and the joys of motherhood that we fail to acknowledge The One who made it all possible.

Take a second and remember the days B.C (Before Children). Remember how you dreamt of this perfect life, being swept off your feet by your prince charming and having beautiful babies to serve as a reminder of your love spilling over in pure bliss? Think about how you two ran through a field of lilies and roses without being scraped or bruised because thorns and arguments didn't exist, only to wake to a completely different reality. For some, this fantasy got close. They got married to their version of prince charming, however, fertility didn't come as easy as one hoped. Then there are those who got the Prince "Charm-is Deceptive" version and may have "put the carriage before the horse." You may be able to identify with either of these examples of these seemingly different women. Although there are differences, I still find that there are more similarities than none. The common thread is the fragility of womanhood desiring wholeness in the family structure.

If you are the mommy who has been graced with the hard task of raising a child(ren) independently, I urge you to be encouraged! God is faithful to do exceedingly and abundantly above and beyond anything you could ever imagine in your life and the life of your child(ren). The great news is that God never said that if you are married, then and only then will your children be considered a gift. His word tells us that all children are gifts from Him and I'm so thankful for this good news because I am a product and an evidence of God's ability to use broken pieces to make a masterpiece.

If you are the mommy who got the spouse of your choice but struggled with fertility in the beginning, remember the days when you wailed before God? Remember the days you prayed without ceasing that God would grant you the deep petition of your heart? Remember how much your faith played tug-of-war with doubt and left you an emotional wreck? Never forget how you knew what you desired was a "tall order" but for God, it was possible!

I remember falling to the floor on my face in reckless abandonment to God for a son. God had blessed my husband and I with two amazingly beautiful daughters, yet there was still this harsh reality that lingered in our lives, which was my husband being the last of his generation to carry his family's name and if God didn't give us a son, the name threatened extinction. There were two mountains that I faced which increased my fears; the risk of carrying a third child after all that I had gone through health-related and the understanding that in the event I manage to conceive, only God could determine the sex.

Now, I want you to recall the moment when God granted your request. Do you remember where you were when you got the phone call or the letter or the ultrasound displaying the tangible answered prayer? Do you remember the overwhelming gratitude that swept over you? It was a place where although you had gotten the greatest news, the focus on the gift gave way to the gratitude that gripped your heart for the Giver. That great place of appreciation is the place I believe God desires for us to revisit often. It is the place in which we not only acknowledge the Giver of all gifts but also understand that without Him, we would have nothing!

Recite this Prayer:

God,

I acknowledge You for being The Great Giver of all gifts. I thank you for the gifts You have so graciously given to me. Father, I appreciate You for all You have done. I pray for Your forgiveness for every time I've placed the gift above You, and for the moments I allowed the business of motherhood to distract me from handling the gifts with proper stewardship. Help me to never be desensitized to Your goodness but remain appreciative of all that You do and have done.

In Jesus name, amen.

SPILL YOUR HEART

_____

_____

_____

_____

_____

_____

_____

_____

_____

_____

DAY 5

LOVE

Love is such a broad subject with so much depth and weight. There are so many great things that are derived from love. Today, I would like to focus on loving our children.

A mother's love transcends all boundaries. I'm reminded of the "prodigal son" as seen in Luke 15: 11-32. This story shows a child who felt they had it all figured out. Of course, this doesn't sound like your teenager, right? In the story, Jesus describes this child as a younger sibling who felt that he could handle his inheritance at a very young age. What I think is most interesting is that the Bible doesn't say the father argued with the child. He simply gave the child what he asked for, even though he knew he couldn't handle it.

The father knew his child may have been irresponsible and lacked good stewardship. He may have felt that not arguing with him and simply letting him go would teach him more than just talking to him could. After being on his own and experiencing the hardships of life, the Bible says that he came to his senses and said, "How many of my father's hired servants have food to spare, and here I am starving to death! I will set out and go back to my father and say to him: Father, I have sinned against heaven and against you. I am no longer worthy to be called your son. Make me like one of your hired servants." So, he got up and went to his father...

This particular passage of scripture offers so much hope. It is such a great moment when one comes to their senses, humbles them self and seeks forgiveness. I believe that the father not only believed the day would come where his son would return, but according to the next passage, he awaited with great anticipation. Luke 15: 20 says, "But while he was still a long way off, his father saw him and was filled with compassion for him; he ran to his son, threw his arms around him and kissed him." This passage doesn't say that the father awaited his son's return with crossed arms and great wrath. It doesn't show a father who felt hopeless either. It didn't say the father sent his son off with great weeping assuming he would never see him again. No! It shows us the great perspective of love from a parent to a child. This passage of scripture demonstrates the weight and effectiveness of a parents love for their child and its power to overcome disobedience, smart mouths, and irrational behaviors. When was the last time you looked past faults and shortcomings and extended love? Sometimes, the greatest discipline is a warm embrace, sweet compassion, and firm love.

Recite this Prayer:

Heavenly Father,

Forgive me for the moments I allow anger to cloud my judgment. You have always been loving and compassionate towards me. Help me to extend that same great love to my child even in their disobedience. God, I believe that You can show them the way and I trust Your great plan for them.

In Jesus Name, Amen.

SPILL YOUR HEART

DAY 6

LOVE

What is unfailing love? It's defined as the reliable, constant, intense feeling of affection that is without error or fault. It is a love we desire to possess as mothers. How perfect the world we live in would be if we all aspired to extend such love. Proverbs 20:6-7 says, "Many claim to have unfailing love, but a faithful person who can find? The righteous lead blameless lives; blessed are their children after them." Although this scripture suggests that no one possess the ability to have unfailing love within themselves, it does offer the sweetest hope that the children of anyone who lives with integrity, the righteous, will be blessed!

It doesn't "just matter" to our children the kind of lifestyle we live, it affects them and their future personally! How we live will ultimately determine if our children will be blessed or not. Therefore, we can never hope to exemplify unfailing love to our children unless we aim to live an intentionally righteous (integral, upright, just, scripturally sound) life. NO PRESSURE MOM! Our healthy decision to live this kind of life assures the blessing over our children. Want to show your children unfailing love? It starts with making the decision in your heart to live by doing what is right because its right, and living your life aimed to please God in everything you do. By doing this, you have given your child an inheritance. They will be called the blessed of the righteous. This can be effective immediately by repenting from all your shortcomings and, as the Bible says, turn from your sinful ways. We may not possess the ability to have unfailing love within us, but if we live right, the Lord will bless our children with His.

Recite this Prayer:

Father God,

I know that apart from You I am nothing. I do not possess the ability to love unfailingly, but with You leading and guiding my life, I can lead a life of integrity. I ask for Your help in this parenting journey and Your blessing over my children.

In Jesus name, Amen.

SPILL YOUR HEART

DAY 7

LOVE

Love is spelled D I S C I P L I N E. This has become such a taboo topic, however, we as moms who love and are dedicated to raising the next generation of believers, citizens, teachers, leaders and politicians should never shy away from discipline.

As a mother, doesn't it feel great when we don't back down from the hard conversations with our kids? Don't we get excited about the lessons we teach them with "time outs" and removing electronics? Sometimes they wear us out, but I tell you from experience that there is no greater euphoria than looking at that cute sweet face and still sticking to your guns of correction! Well mamas I got good news and bad news. Good news is, you are doing a great job instilling structure and order into your children's lives. Bad news is, you haven't uprooted the foolishness. It has only subsided for a moment. According to scripture, our love is better displayed when we do the thing that we mostly dread; physical discipline! Proverbs 22:15 says, "A youngster's heart is filled with foolishness, but physical discipline will drive it far away."

Just because we have to use physical discipline verses a painless timeout, doesn't mean we can't reinforce love with tenderness. In fact, I find that the sweetest most heartfelt embraces typically follow the hard moments of discipline. I truly believe all discipline should be reinforced with a warm sincere touch. It is a moment that is vulnerable and a moment where both mommy and child are transparent and open. It is a moment where our children are susceptible to instruction and therefore are most teachable. In our house, we make sure to "finish the love", which means we have our moment of discipline, we let them cry and give them a moment, and then we have them come back (now a days, they naturally come back on their own) and we hold them, explain why they got the spanking, explain what they should do better next time, and then we seal it ALWAYS with "I love yous" and hugs and tons of kisses.

As mothers, it is our job to show love even when it's tough and when we feel quite faint in doing so. We are responsible for teaching our children what is right and driving this foolishness out of them. The Bible says in Proverbs 13:24, "Those who spare the rod of discipline hate their children. Those who love their children care enough to discipline them." Correcting our children through physical discipline can be tough, but the Bible tells us that this act of Love proves we truly care for them.

Recite this Prayer:

Father God,

Help me to love my children in a caring way. Enable me to teach them according to Your will. Give me strength to stick to my guns and to physically discipline my children with the understanding that the discomfort I hate to see them in is a small price to pay to kill the root of foolishness in their heart. Remind me in times of weakness that you know what's best and I can't go wrong if I follow your lead as it pertains to the life of my children.

In Jesus name, Amen.

SPILL YOUR HEART

_____

_____

_____

_____

_____

_____

_____

_____

_____

_____

_____

_____

_____

_____

DAY 8

LOVE

1 Corinthians 13:4-8 says, "Love is patient, love is kind. It does not envy, it does not boast, it is not proud. It does not dishonor others, it is not self-seeking, it is not easily angered, it keeps no record of wrongs. Love does not delight in evil but rejoices with the truth." This is the love that the Father desires for us to have. The several characteristics mentioned in this scripture challenge us to lead a life loving with pure selflessness. It also invites us to parent in such a manner that is uncommon amongst our culture. God's word challenges our mere understanding of love. This love once applied gives us an immense depth of character. The love God desires us to have for our children and others transcends all the shortcomings and flaws they may have. It is this love that corrects me when I grow impatient with my toddler. It matures my endurance when I've asked my adolescent daughter to do the same thing innumerous times, repetitively, over

and over again, daily without getting my expected results instantaneously! This love quickens me especially when I have a newborn who seemingly cries without end, even when I've done all I know to do to comfort him. The love the Apostle Paul speaks of in this scripture helps widen my perspective, broaden my shoulders and makes me sure-footed to support the weight of the task God has entrusted to me as their mother. I encourage you today, mothers, to relentlessly chase your children down and overpower them with this love...

Recite this Prayer:

Father God,

Teach me how to love with the love shown in 1 Corinthians 13. Help me to be selfless with the way I love. My desire is to please You with how I love my children and others. Help me to exercise this love with not only my little people but with everyone I encounter.

In Jesus name, Amen.

SPILL YOUR HEART

_____

_____

_____

_____

_____

_____

_____

_____

_____

_____

_____

_____

_____

_____

_____

_____

DAY 9

BEATING DEPLETION

As a mother who would give her very last bite of food to her children and take the clothes off her very own back to clothe them, it is hard to fathom how those precious little gifts (children) can take that food and take those clothes and ask for more. We give time and effort and tears and sweat and somewhere in our hearts, we hope that our 3-year-old can see the sacrifices and give us a little pat on the back, understanding a little bit of what it takes to make the daily grind work... nope! They suck the energy right out of us and typically with a crazy straw... then they ask for seconds.

If we pay close attention, our children can teach us just how selfish we are as human beings by nature. They teach us how our flesh is never satisfied and how after when we seemingly get what we want, we quickly grow bored and subsequently want more. If you are anything like me, you would continue giving until you have nothing left to offer. This is the base and foundation of our problem.

We should never give until we have nothing left. How can we continue to be a great example, role model, teacher, confidant, support system to others, a mother to our babies a wife to our husbands, a friend to our girlfriends if we give all we have and have nothing left to give? Remember this... sacrifice doesn't always mean depletion! Give until you feel like you have made a sacrifice but if your giving drains the life out of you and puts you in a bad mood or mindset, you have become weary. You are giving until you are too weak to be of any good to anyone or even yourself. You have exerted yourself excessively. The Bible says in Galatians 6:9, "Let us not become weary in doing good, for at the proper time we will reap a harvest if we do not give up." This scripture offers so much encouragement because it licenses us to give and do in increments suggesting that we do good but don't overdo it. We should give to our children according to our measurement and when we feel the faintness rising, we should take a break and remember the joy that awaits us on the other end of this giving. This particular scripture gives us hope that the good we do, and the sacrifices we make to ensure a better future for our children will bring forth much fruit if we are not overtaken by depletion.

Recite this Prayer:

Dear Heavenly Father,

Help me to plug into you and be sourced. God, I rely on You for wisdom, energy, understanding, patience, and peace in raising the beautiful children You have given me. You, Lord, are my guide and my light. Give me clarity on what is my measurement and help me to give the proper dosages of me to each of my children. I look forward to the hope that is found in Your word that reminds me of the reward of sacrifice and doing good. I live with great expectation to see the fruit of my labor as I reap a great harvest of seeing the results of this hard work. One day I believe my children will rise up, finally see the sacrifice, and they will call me blessed. Bless them now with the foundation of strength and courage to one day have the privilege to give in great measure to their own children.

In Jesus Name, Amen.

SPILL YOUR HEART

_____

_____

_____

_____

_____

_____

_____

_____

_____

_____

_____

_____

_____

_____

DAY 10

BEATING DEPLETION

O ften, when tending to the cares of this world that makes us responsible and healthy adults/mommies, we lose sight of tending to our own mental stability and forget about the joys and healing powers of peace. We spend so much time being caretakers that we forget to take care of ourselves.

Philippians 4:6-7 says, "Don't worry about anything; instead, pray about everything. Tell God what you need and thank Him for all He has done. Then, you will experience God's peace which exceeds anything we can understand. His peace will guard your hearts and minds as you live in Christ Jesus."

What I love about this scripture is that it gives us both hope and direction. It gives us instructions in order to obtain and sustain our mental health. The Apostle Paul, the writer of these profound words found in the book of Philippians, leads with the encouragement to not worry, knowing that life experiences can yield much concern. He then instructs us on how to take our attention off our current issue, mundane routines, and our circumstances by praying/talking to God about them. When we turn off our social media notifications and mute our phones in the midst of hardship and begin to talk to God about what troubles us instead of running to our peers, we acknowledge that He is the great counselor and His resources are stronger than whatever situation we face. We gain confidence through the knowledge that He is able to fix the situations in which we lack control.

The writer continues to give us direction on how to maintain our mental health/stability by redirecting our attention to a state of remembrance. He instructs us to look back over our lives and remember all that God has done. When we do this, it instantly puts us in a state of thanksgiving, where the peace of God is made available to us, knowing once again that he's done it once and he's able to help us again. It is in this state that we draw from the rich well of confidence in God who is more than able to do anything and is sure to never fail! His countless victories give us the peace we need in our hearts and minds to continue to conquer our today.

Let this peace overtake your minds during the business of life. Allow this peace to replenish your mind from the things that may have left you feeling drained and mentally depleted.

Recite this Prayer:

Father God,

I thank and praise You simply for being who You are. You have never failed me. Thank you for all that You have done in my life. I pray for strength to make it through this journey called life and seek You whole-heartedly for mental stability and peace in the midst of life's roughest storms and same ole same ole routines. Be glorified in and through my life Father. You have always come through and I'm never far from Your peace.

In Jesus name, Amen.

SPILL YOUR HEART

DAY 11

BEATING DEPLETION

Oftentimes, when we as mothers desire to provide a lifestyle for our children we could have only dreamed of, we exhaust ourselves to ensure that such vision comes to pass. We understand that in order to achieve our various visions, we must set goals. We forget in the journey towards these goals, however, the importance of coming up for air.

Proverbs 16:3 says, "Commit your actions to the Lord, and your plans will succeed." Although goal setting is vital to leading a healthy life of intentional pursuit of purpose, it is absolutely imperative that we take breaks/days off. These breaks offer us opportunities to regroup, refocus, and reset. Taking these "intentional" days off aids us in beating the depletion that can come with the desire to make strides of excellence. Do not allow depletion to interfere with you meeting the goals you've set for your family or yourself. Pace yourself with those earlier mentioned breaks. Let them fuel you in the pursuit of your goals. Allow your goals to drive you to the desired destination but don't hesitate to stop at a gas station or a few restaurants on your way there. Remember; it will happen for you and for your family. The journey is always the best part of the destination.

Recite this Prayer:

Heavenly Father,

I pray for the tenacity and endurance to achieve the goals I've set for myself and my family. I ask that You direct my steps in this pursuit of accomplishment with excellence. I pray that you take away the guilt that is commonly associated with taking breaks. I submit my plans and goals to You.

In Jesus name, Amen.

SPILL YOUR HEART

DAY 12

BEATING DEPLETION

I've found that the best way to beat the feeling of being drained, which causes a lack of motivation or the ability to dream, is to put the things that inspire me to live a purpose-filled life before my eyes. It is truly vital for us to keep the vision we have for our lives visible. Hang on to the scriptures that motivate you, inspire you and drive you back into destiny. I mean scriptures like Romans 8:37 that says, "... in all these things we are more than conquerors through him who loved us" or like Philippians 4:13, "I can do all this through him who gives me strength." Truths like these give us the spiritual recharge we need to continue to win in life! These are promises that have and still are getting me through every storm that blows my way. They give me the power I need to speak to the wind and the waves with authority from heaven. Scriptures like these remind us that we are not failures when we haven't reached our vision, but we are indeed overcomers and more than conquerors! Some strive for victory but in the eyes of God and in the way, he's set us up as believers in this world, we fight FROM victory. You may ask, "If that be true, then how can we fail?" Failing is something we've all experienced, but being a failure is not who we are! We are children of God and therefore, we win! Begin to live your life not toward victory, but from victory! Get that vision clear and keep it in front of your eyes. It makes it easier to live on purpose. Once you get the vision, you never lose focus. You got this mama!

Recite this prayer:

Dear Heavenly Father,

Give me ears to hear Your word, eyes to see Your purpose for my life and a heart to believe that all Your promises are for me. I surrender my plans to You Lord and ask that Your perfect will be done in my life. I want to see clear. I need your help with vision. Help me stay focused.

In Jesus name, Amen.

SPILL YOUR HEART

DAY 13

BEAUTY

When was the last time you looked in the mirror and took an in-depth look at yourself and saw all the beauty that radiates from the inside out?! The older I get the more I realize that beauty cannot only be defined by the outward appearance. It is an inward quality that encapsulates responsibility, respect, integrity, humility, authenticity, and selflessness. Such qualities shine brightest from within and make us the beautiful women God created us to be.

I believe that our children see us in this light from the time they first hear our voice. According to my children, I am the world's greatest chef even if peanut butter and jelly sandwiches are the only thing on the menu. To them, I am funny when I am having a rather goofy and awkwardly quirky day. My children even make me feel like maybe my poop doesn't stink or their tolerance is matchless because they certainly don't mind hanging out in the bathroom with me for the entire time. I say some of these things humorously, however, I truly believe that we should see ourselves through the lens of our children and their thoughts about us. When you look in the mirror, begin to see yourself the way your children see you. They don't see an exhausted, no makeup wearing, may not be at the desired weight, overworked mommy. All they see is strength, funny, and the qualities that make us beautiful great moms.

I want you to take a second, go to the mirror, and look again. Look deeper this time. Look until you can't see what you always see. Stare into your eyes and hear your children's voice say, "Thank you mommy... you're the best. I love you mommy. You look pretty mommy." That's the voice that matters. Those are the ones who know beauty first hand. Don't get stuck on your definition of beauty. The true attributes will come from the little ones we love.

Recite this Prayer:

Dear Heavenly Father,

Help me to accept and embrace that I am beautiful. Thank You, Lord, for gracing me with all the qualities that truly make me beautiful. Thank You for making me more than enough. Also, help me to never lose sight of your Word that says that I am fearfully and wonderfully made in Your image (Psalm 139:14).

In Jesus name, Amen.

SPILL YOUR HEART

_____

_____

_____

_____

_____

_____

_____

_____

_____

_____

_____

_____

_____

_____

_____

DAY 14

BEAUTY

Ever wanted to know what the true essence of beauty entails? We know that society has made it annoyingly clear of its definition of beauty which seems to be incredibly specific and oftentimes discriminative. We see these incredibly physically attractive people when we open magazines and as we drive down the road, their photos are larger than life plastered on billboards. I'm sure it's not for the purpose of making those of us who look different feel less beautiful, but if we are honest with ourselves, we can attest to the fact that we sometimes allow these images to taint the way we see ourselves. We allow these images to set a false standard of what beauty really is. The images that pop up when we search for beauty in our search engines could very well be a part of it, however, the part that is not mentioned is that beauty has many facets. Beauty cannot be fully grasped in one picture, one poster board, one magazine or even one's reflection in the mirror! Although all these things capture a snapshot of what beauty indeed is, they cannot define the true essence of beauty.

Proverbs 31:25 says, "She is clothed with strength and dignity." It speaks of the true essence of beauty being character, which is something far greater than physical appearance

Proverbs 31:30 says, "Charm is deceptive, and beauty is fleeting, but a woman who fears the Lord is to be praised." This scripture proves that smooth words and a pretty face are no match for a woman who honors God! It is the interweaving of a woman's soul (her mind, will, and emotions) interlocking with the Spirit of God that makes up the true essence of her beauty.

I love that the word of God defines the depths of beauty as characteristics and not limit it to the shallow, ever-changing reflection in the mirror. Sometimes I don't feel or look so pretty, but I sure am glad that my beauty is more than skin deep. Be encouraged today, mama, that when you honor God, He says that you are praise worthy. Honor God today.

Recite this Prayer:

Dear Heavenly Father,

Help me to see myself the way You see me. Help me to dare to go deeper and explore Your spirit. I invite Your spirit to dwell on the inside of me. My soul interlocking with Your Spirit makes me truly beautiful and worthy of praise. I love you.

In Jesus name, Amen.

SPILL YOUR HEART

_____

_____

_____

_____

_____

_____

_____

_____

_____

_____

_____

_____

_____

_____

_____

_____

DAY 15

BEAUTY

1 Peter 3:3-4 says, "Your beauty should not come from outward adornments, such as elaborate hairstyles and the wearing of gold jewelry or fine clothes. Rather, it should be that of your inner self, the unfading beauty of a gentle and quiet spirit, which is of great worth in God's sight."

The older I get the more I realize how meaningless superficial things truly are. When I was younger, I cared a great deal about designer labels. I had to wear some sort of brand to feel validated among my peers. As I grew up and moved out of my mother's home, I realized that the more, mature, crowd I surrounded myself with cared less and less about brands and saw clothes and shoes as necessities which they purchased not for who designed them, but for what they were designed for! It was an entirely new experience for me. It opened my eyes to a broader perspective to see things the way they should be and not take on the perspective of what some may have projected onto me.

I love 1 Peter 3:3-4 so much because it deals with a heart condition. I'm sure Peter, the author responsible for writing these profound words, was not writing them with the intent to "bash" a woman from desiring to adorn herself with such accessories for the purpose of being beautiful. I believe he was shedding light on an underlying issue which had to do with dressing up or covering up insecurities. I believe he saw a society of women like we see today who thought they must put on all these things to feel beautiful. I know I'm guilty of not feeling really secure when I'm not wearing makeup, and Lord knows I love a good pair of heels! Are these things wrong to enjoy? Of course not! Peter was simply informing us that our worth is far greater than anything we could wear. He explained that true beauty is not a look but a characteristic. It is a heart condition.

How does your heart look? When was the last time you examined your heart? If God were to search it what would He find? Would He find a woman with a meek and humble disposition? Would He find someone who promotes peace and love? If not, let us take our insecurities, self-doubts, and other inner filth before God and ask Him to cleanse us. Let's allow Him to purify our souls (our mind, our will, and our emotions) and give us unfading beauty from within.

Today, I want to dare you… no… double dare you… no no no… DOUBLE DOG DARE YOU to get ready for your day, and then when you are satisfied, begin to remove one accessory a day until you can walk out the house raw, bold and beautiful. You can do it. When you can accept yourself with nothing to assist you, you have reached a new level of beauty.

Recite this prayer:

Dear Heavenly Father,

Search my heart. If there is anything that flaws my character, I ask that You remove it. Give me a great wealth of character which is true beauty.

In Jesus name, Amen.

SPILL YOUR HEART

DAY 16

BEAUTY

Psalm 139: 14 says, "I praise you because I am fearfully and wonderfully made; your works are wonderful, I know that full well." When we realize that we are made in the image of God, we will begin to understand better the fullness of beauty (Gen 1:27). We can gain confidence in knowing that our Heavenly Father has handcrafted us perfectly. There's no other thing in creation that God shaped with His hands. No other creation has the highest level of authority over the earth like we do. What a magnificent honor! Being made in the image of God the Father is a truth, reminding us that we really do possess never ending, unfading beauty. The God of Heaven who holds the power to speak life into nothing and it comes to be, thought enough of us to form us not with His words, but with His hands. Ephesians 2:10 says, "For we are God's handiwork, created in Christ Jesus to do good works, which God prepared in advance for us to do."

I believe when we accept that we are all created in the image AND LIKENESS of God, we can more easily accept the truth that we are naturally beautiful. We must accept this quickly because the bible confirms our beauty and then tells us to get rolling on to the work God has set up for us to do. Don't get lost in the pressures of beauty and redefining beauty and finding the unique you to the point of not doing the good work God has made us to do. Get up, get confident, and get to work girl!!

Recite this prayer:

Father God,

Thank You for taking Your time on me. You handcrafted me with purpose, with hope and You have given me a future. I ask that You allow me to better walk in my purpose. Give me a community that will cultivate the call You have placed on my life because when I am walking in my divine purpose, I am walking in the fullness of beauty.

In Jesus name, Amen.

SPILL YOUR HEART

DAY 17

BEAUTY

Did you know that the perception of beauty is truly a heart condition? Don't allow the perception of others to determine if the beauty you possess is validated. We all have our perceptions of beauty; however, the most important perception is the truth and the truth is found in God's word. When God created all things including mankind, He determined that every single detail was good and would give Him glory (Genesis 1:1-31). Therefore, others perception of our appearance remains void.

There is one thing that determines our true beauty in God's eyes, and that is an upright heart before Him that is pure and holy. 1 Samuel 16:7 says, "But the Lord said to Samuel, "Do not consider his appearance or his height, for I have rejected him. The Lord does not look at the things people look at. People look at the outward appearance, but the Lord looks at the heart."

Let us consider our heart before we get dressed in our finest attire and make sure it is pure at all times, honest and selfless before our God. Our heart defines our character and our character can be more attractive than the most beautiful garment. Let your beauty radiate from within and bring God the ultimate glory.

Recite this Prayer:

Dear Heavenly Father,

I ask that You purify my heart. Make me clean. Give me the beauty that shines from within. May the words of my mouth and the meditation of my heart be pleasing to you, O Lord, my rock and my redeemer (Psalm 19:14).

In Jesus name, Amen.

SPILL YOUR HEART

DAY 18

INSPIRATION

Are you feeling a bit burned out from the seemingly never-ending cycle of routine? Do you lack energy or motivation to work toward your goals and dreams? Do you feel so bogged down by the weight of your responsibilities that you feel lost creatively? If so, you are NOT alone!

As a stay at home mom that homeschools her three children among other responsibilities, it is very difficult to carve out the time required to be creative or simply pursue some personal goals, dreams, or hobbies at times. Though it is very difficult to manage a busy life and excel at achieving goals, it is not out of the realm of possibilities. It can, in fact, be done with proper planning and prioritizing.

Becoming successful at accomplishing goals starts with the inspiration. Think about the thing(s) that inspire you. Take a mental snapshot. Now, take the next step to bring those thoughts into reality. Surf the web and print out pictures. Create a vision board with your goal(s) in mind and hang them up. Keep the vision in plain sight. Habakkuk 2:2-3 says, "Then the Lord replied: Write down the revelation (goal, vision) and make it plain on tablets so that a herald may run with it. For the revelation awaits an appointed time, it speaks of the end and will not prove false. Though it linger, wait for it; it will certainly come and will not delay."

In order to accomplish dreams, we must first establish what they look like. For instance, if one desires to be the fastest runner in the world, then they must first find the fastest runner in the world currently. After finding that Usain Bolt holds the record, one can then obtain an understanding of the goal they wish to accomplish. It gives them a "start to finish-line" awareness.

There has NEVER been a quick or instantaneous fix in accomplishing goals. It is a marathon and not a sprint (no pun intended). The journey between inspiration and accomplishing goals is vital. It is not for the faint of heart. It requires great sacrifice. This sacrifice includes giving up what you love for the things you love most. Accomplishing your goals requires hard work, determination, loss of sleep and in some cases loneliness. Oftentimes in my journey, I discover that the discipline required for me to take the next step isn't always popular and can subsequently make me feel lonely in the pursuit of my goals. When my husband and I decided to go vegan, it was definitely not popular, neither was it an easy transition, however, it was necessary for the goals we set for our family.

What I'm trying to say is "do it alone!" Do it even if it takes all of your friends and family a while to catch up to the change. Do it even if it doesn't make a bit of sense to anyone else. Think about the things that inspire you the most and while pursuing, never lose sight of them. KEEP THE VISION IN FRONT OF YOU. ONCE YOU GET THE VISION, YOU'LL NEVER LOSE FOCUS!

Recite this Prayer:

Dear Heavenly Father,

I submit my plans, goals and dreams to You. I ask that You align them with Your will and purpose for my life. God, give me the inspiration and time I currently lack to pursue my goals and I ask for Your help in accomplishing them all.

In Jesus name, Amen.

SPILL YOUR HEART

DAY 19

INSPIRATION

Inspiration is the process of being mentally stimulated to feel or do something unique and creative.

When was the last time you challenged yourself creatively? I mean when was the last time you took time to cultivate your God-given talents and/or gifts? I feel that this topic of inspiration is necessary for our journey called life. We all possess special gifts even if these gifts are hidden treasures still locked up on the inside of us waiting for something like today's devotional to shed light on it, in hopes of awakening those places of untapped potential. We were created by The Creator of creativity, whose signature is on the horizon, the mountains, the hills, the seas, the stars, and the clouds. The bible tells us that all His creation speaks of His glory.

Ever been to a beach? It is my favorite place. It is one of the things I love most about living in Florida. While standing on the beach, I love the feeling of the warm, soft sand between my toes. I love watching the birds fly just above the water and looking out as far as my eyes can see and still not being able to tell where the sea ends and the sky begins. I love to close my eyes and hear the roaring yet calming sound of the sea as the waves crash against the shore. There is nothing like a cool breeze in the midst of a warm beach day. All these things were designed for us to draw from rich inspiration. They stimulate our mind, body, and soul.

Being made in His likeness (Genesis 1:27), there is no wonder why we feel this common and natural longing to create. I've noticed lack of inspiration, sadness, worthlessness and just feeling lost when trying to be creative without surrounding myself with affirming messages and pictures that encapsulate the things that inspire me. We need a constant reminder of our natural God given ability to create and be creative. Let's be intentional about seeking inspiration in our everyday surroundings. Inspiration is important because it keeps the mind from idleness. Inspiration is also known as "a spark." I like to think of its importance as my mind staying out of the dark. We all know dark is associated with death and all things no one wants. Inspiration births creativity, so it's important to create and be creative because it simply keeps our minds out of the dark places. Allow the wonders of this world on your ride to work or church or school to remind you that you were created in the likeness of the Master Creator. Today, CREATE!!! Look at Gods creation and be inspired!

Recite this Prayer:

Lord,

Thank You for sparking an all-consuming blaze of inspiration in me. I thank You Lord, for unlocking the gifts and abilities that You have placed within me. I pray for an unquenchable fire of creativity to burn long after this moment of inspiration subsides.

In Jesus name, Amen.

SPILL YOUR HEART

DAY 20

INSPIRATION

The difference between a goal and a dream is a date. The moment we give our dream a deadline, it becomes a goal. Goals are accomplished by living in the direction of the target. For instance, if I dream to be a licensed cosmetologist, I would first find the average time of training completion. Then, I would set both, a date to start training, and the date I would like to have the license in hand. I would then follow the criteria of training, focusing on the final date to make sure I keep my eyes on the prize.

What determines my success after my enrollment is CONSISTENCY. Consistency is the secret ingredient to accomplishing any and every goal. Consistency is the ability to see the goal date through every storm and every trial. You cannot make it through even the smallest issue if you don't have consistency. Nothing of a great value comes easy. Everything of great value comes only with consistency.

We must have the work ethic it takes to become a success by our own measurement of what success is. Success, for me, is creating goals for myself and my family (such as entrepreneurial, educational, and health and wellness). These goals infuse purpose into my veins and gives me the jolt I need to stay motivated at all times. Proverbs 16:3 says, "Commit to the Lord whatever you do, and he will establish your plans." As you make strides to dream and accomplish goals, remember that what we consider goals are only farfetched dreams if they don't have a date and if we don't have a plan for them. Today, look through your yesteryears and think of those dreams that now seem impossible or long gone. Grab a tablet, hop online, and research what it takes to accomplish said dream. By the end of the day, create a 6 to 12 month plan on your next steps to those dreams. If you know where you want to be in 12 months, then you know where you have to be in 6 months. If you know where you must be in 6 months, then you know where you should be by month 3. After you write this out, pray over it, and take the first step… why are you still reading this? GO!! Turn those dreams into GOALS.

Recite this prayer:

Dear Heavenly Father,

I ask for the tenacity and consistency to chase down every dream until I completely overtake and accomplish them all. Help me to manage the time it takes to accomplish each goal and give me the strength to endure through any trial.

In Jesus name, Amen.

SPILL YOUR HEART

_____

_____

_____

_____

_____

_____

_____

_____

_____

_____

_____

_____

_____

_____

_____

DAY 21

INSPIRATION

2 Timothy 3:16-17 says, "All Scripture is God-breathed and is useful for teaching, rebuking, correcting and training in righteousness, so that the servant of God may be thoroughly equipped for every good work."

To know that every word written in such a sacred book that we are privileged to have access to here in America is all God influenced is the biggest inspiration we could ever have as believers. God desires a relationship with us so much so, that He created a manuscript to help us stay focused, on track, spiritually empowered, and safe in every season of our life. The bible teaches us how to fight, how to love, how to have discipline, integrity and above all, the bible gives us hope! Hope for a better day during our trials, hope that there is more beyond what we can physically see, and hope that one day we will be united both with our Heavenly Father and with those loved ones who have gone on before us.

What greater inspiration is there than Gods word? The guidance we need, the structure we're always trying to maintain, the answers we can never find, the guilt free "spanking your kids is good for them" stuff is all in this great manual. Everything we need is in the word of God.

Go to "Proverbs" and start reading some great inserts on wisdom. Start at chapter 1 and everyday read a little more and a little more. It is "PACKED FULL" with great information that can be applied immediately and bring inspiration to your heart and home. Write your favorite scriptures and notes on the pages to follow.

Recite this Prayer:

Dear Heavenly Father,

I thank You for the word and the all-inspiring wisdom it pours into me. Help me follow your instructions and continue to guide me with the light of this word in the darker places of motherhood. Thank You for the hope you have given me. I aim to allow your word to be a lamp to my feet and a light to my path. I will read your word and hide it in my heart as my inspiration to stay focused, stay hopeful and stay on the right path as a mother to my children. I'm forever grateful for this help.

In Jesus name, Amen.

SPILL YOUR HEART

DAY 22

MOTIVATION

Motivation... to answer your question, no. No, we did not spend the last couple of days on motivation. We spent the last four days becoming motivated by inspiration. Although inspiration and motivation are complementary, they are not the same. Let's unpack this for a clearer understanding.

Inspiration is the process of being mentally stimulated to do or feel something, especially to do something creative. Motivation is based on the reason or reasons one has for acting or behaving in a particular way. Inspiration is a spark that brings about a spontaneous act while motivation is a well thought out motive behind an action. Both are sudden sparks that lead us to action, however, motivation will keep us going in the direction of purpose. Inspiration will spark a flame, but motivation will keep it burning.

What motivates us most is experience. Our life experiences give us reason to passionately pursue purpose. Dare I say, motivation holds more weight than inspiration because what inspires us in a moment can easily lose its momentum as it is led by feelings. When we lack strong feelings about a thought, task, or goal, that thought, task or goal runs the risk of dying just as prematurely as it is birthed. Motivation, however, is rooted and grounded upon the solidarity of experience. I'll explain.

I may be inspired to paint a picture when there is an easel set up with a blank canvas before me. If when I look to my left there are brushes and, on my right, a beautiful multicolor palette accompanied with a view, in that instant, I am inspired by all of the resources accessible to me. The problem arises when the time comes to leave. As soon as I walk out the door, the opportunity is also created for the inspiration to leave as well.

What inspiration lacks that motivation encapsulates is consistency. It is the burning desire to carry out the foundation of a matter. Any successful athlete, if asked why they play any sport with such passion, agility and endurance, would attest to being moved by reason. Whether this reason is providing a legacy for their family, or securing a healthy retirement, these reasons are the motives that fuel their motivation to accomplish their goal.

Did you know that God's love for us is His motive to relentlessly pursue us?! John 3:16 says, "For God so loved the world that He gave His one and only Son, that whoever believes in Him shall not perish but have eternal life." This love is best translated in John 15:13 that says, "Greater love has no one than this: to lay down one's life for one's friends." Talk about the greatest display of motivation!

As a child I can recall my mom taking my siblings and I on great family vacations. We hardly ever ate out because there was always a home cooked meal on the table. She would throw us the best parties on a budget all while selling fish and chicken platters, candy and snacks to the neighborhood for extra income. My mom managed to do all these things while somehow balancing jobs and paying bills not to mention keeping my siblings and I safe in the "hoods" of St. Louis, MO. She wanted so badly for us to have more and to see more of the world and to have great opportunities beyond the drug infested streets of "da Lou" but she did all that her capacity would allow. Today, I use my mom's hopes for us and my upbringing as my motive. I've never been motivated by anyone more than my mom. She has helped me to home school my kids and encouraged me to pursue higher education. As a result of that encouragement I am the first female of my generation to obtain a college degree. If it had not been for my mom "dragging" me to church I would not be the woman of God I am today nor would I have been in a place where the greatest God-fearing man could find me. The blessings I have the privilege of considering "normal" are actually the results of the drive that was birthed in me through the motivation of the memories of my early childhood. Had she only inspired me with emotion and great words, I would have forgotten it all in the noise of walking into adulthood. Instead, she gave me a reason to want more for my life, and for my children's life.

What is your reason? Why do you mother the way you do? Today, write out that reason. Remember the reason you go so hard for them. When you think through those reasons and you write them down, keep them in the front of your mind and never ever allow yourself to forget why.

Recite this Prayer:

Dear Heavenly Father,

I thank You for giving me the greatest example of motivation. Some of us may have been blessed to have parents like mine who have given us a motive to do more, believe more and hope for more, but what I'm most grateful for is that You gave us all Your son who sacrificed it all for us which gives us the motivation to do the same for others. I pray I create a strong foundation for my children to not only be inspired but to have a reason to exceed all my accomplishments.

In Jesus name, Amen.

SPILL YOUR HEART

DAY 23

MOTIVATION

Do you have a routine? What are some of the things you do to ensure that your children have the best start to their adulthood? As mothers, we only have eighteen years to make the most impacting life-altering decisions for our children's future (No pressure, right?!). Setting goals for your family, whether it is academically, spiritually, physically, financially or recreational, will help keep stress down and our confidence up.

The decisions we make as moms determine the appetite our children will have for their life. What we practice and how we operate will oftentimes be the foundation of how our children will operate as they go on in life. If we read a lot (even if it's just by nature and not by hobby), there is a strong chance that our children could form a taste for literature and give them a craving to dig deeper into the world of reading, writing, and becoming a student of wisdom. Our tenacity to provide a well-balanced diet can give them a taste bud for physical health. We as moms introduce fun ideas such as becoming "tooth fairies" to teach our children to save and/or invest, and it gives them a healthy understanding of reaping and sowing. As a mom who homeschools, I realize that routine not only provides consistency, it also provides structure. It instills organization which is extremely important because the lack thereof breeds disorder.

My very first job was working with "troubled" kids in the inner city of, my home town, St. Louis, Mo. There, I learned that children actually are not really "troubled" but rather they have become a product of their environment. Most children who fall subject to their environment fall due to a lack of structure. A structured life is not only healthy for children's development, it is also what the children desire. In working there, I found that rules were something kids barked at, but also something that made them very proud to obey when followed up with both discipline and reward.

Set daily goals. Create a doable routine. This will provide consistency and structure. It can get mundane, but it is better than disorder. If our kids build their life with a foundation of what they see us do, it's very important that they are motivated by order, and structure.

Recite this Prayer:

Dear Heavenly Father,

I pray for the tenacity and structure it takes to produce the next God-fearing generation. Give me the patience I need to create and stick to a schedule that will be most beneficial and healthy for my family.

In Jesus name, Amen.

SPILL YOUR HEART

DAY 24

MOTIVATION

Then Jesus said, "Come to me, all of you who are weary and carry heavy burdens, and I will give you rest. Take my yoke upon you. Let me teach you because I am humble and gentle at heart, and you will find rest for your souls. For my yoke is easy to bear, and the burden I give you is light." (Matthew 11:28-30).

Sometimes, it is hard to be motivated when life has weighed us down with the grave responsibility to be healthy adults and above average moms. When life throws a hearty portion of cares on you, the best thing to do is be refreshed in God's word. Allow God's truth to be the reason you get out of bed and place one foot in front of the other. 1 Peter 5:7 says it best. "Give all your worries and cares to God, for He cares about you." When we rest in the truth of God's promises found in His word, we can become motivated by the hope it gives us and press on toward our goals.

Truths like Philippians 4:13 that says, "For I can do everything through Christ, who gives me strength." Truths like Romans 8:37 that says, "In all things we are more than conquerors through him who loves us."

Today, find a scripture to rest in. Lay down or sit back and put your feet up. Find a scripture and some ice-cream and REST in the comfort of sure promises and the cotton like fluffiness of soft-serve.

Recite this Prayer:

Father, God

I give You the anxiety, stress, sadness, and heaviness the world has burdened me with. I exchange it for Your burden that is light and Your yoke that is easy. God thank You for Your promises that gives me reason and tenacity to move forward with Holy boldness. I thank You that Your word says that You will never leave me nor forsake me. What a promise to lay hold of. Your promises spark a flame within me that can never be extinguished.

In Jesus name, Amen.

SPILL YOUR HEART

_____

_____

_____

_____

_____

_____

_____

_____

_____

_____

_____

_____

_____

DAY 25

MOTIVATION

Let's take a moment to breathe in deeply the goodness The Lord has shown to us. Whether in a near-death experience, a child being rescued from a harmful situation, the doctor confirming a fresh bill of health, or whatever the experience, let's take a second and remember that moment in time. If God has shown Himself to be faithful in your life, if you can reflect and point out memories where He's been your deliverer or your protection, or your provider, then you have great means for unbreakable sure motivation.

When God spared my life after I fell out of a moving vehicle and slammed my head against a boulder causing me to have blood pour into the back of my cracked skull, or the time God saved me when a miscarriage gone wrong (as if a miscarriage isn't bad enough) poisoned my blood stream giving me only six hours to live, I saw God more as a sustainer and protector and deliverer.

This makes it easy for me to be motivated in areas where I need similar intervention. My testimonies are the reason I can climb myself out of the little chasms of fear that try to swallow me whole. I guess you can say they are my motive to push beyond the fear that comes and the doubts I create. I reach back to these memories and I say if God did it before, he can do it again.

God is never changing! WHAT JOY!!! Mothers in the "black church" use to sing a song that said, "Hold to God's unchanging hand." Let God's unchanging character motivate you to trust Him more. Allow your experiences to set a fire inside you to start the one thing you have been dreaming to accomplish but haven't had the courage to yet. Never lose sight of the hope we have found in God through Him providing what we've needed in our past. God is the great motivator. Let him prove that to you as you wake up in the morning before you get the kids ready for the day!

Recite this Prayer:

God,

I thank You for all the times You have kept me. I ask for the faith to believe that the same power that delivered me from danger, can also deliver me from the fear and doubt that tries to pollute my thoughts. Deliver me from the doubt that tells me I will never be more than just a dreamer. Deliver me from the fear of actually succeeding. God, my desire is to trust You more.

In Jesus name, Amen.

SPILL YOUR HEART

DAY 26

INTENTIONAL PRAYER

Prayer is sincerely one of my favorite things to do. I love that the Father longs to hear from His children. There is nothing He wouldn't do for us and like any good father, He will spare no expense in rescuing His children. I love that when I call on Him, He shows Himself strong in life situations and circumstances on my behalf. I believe that's one of the several reasons why the enemy tries his very best to make us feel too drained and defeated to pray. The enemy knows the power you and I possess just by simply getting into the presence of God. Psalm 16:11 says, "You make known to me the path of life; in your presence, there is fullness of joy; at your right hand are pleasures forevermore." What great promises we look forward to in God's presence.

Let nothing stop you from approaching the throne of grace through prayer and let us linger in His presence with great expectation! When we experience the joys and regenerating power of God that are found in His presence, we will be renewed and refreshed. When we pray to our Father and trust with boldness that he will hear us and run to us, we will demolish every devil that tries to hinder us. Pray often and stay engulfed in His presence!

Recite this Prayer:

Dear Heavenly Father,

I thank You for making Your presence available to me. I thank You for giving me the peace that surpasses all understanding and a hope that cannot be shaken! Accept this time of intentional prayer Father.

In Your son Jesus' name I pray, Amen.

SPILL YOUR HEART

DAY 27

INTENTIONAL PRAYER

I believe we are our best to others when we are able to give from our overflow. The way to access this overflow is through intentional prayer. If we lack patience, time, and energy we should pray and ask God for these things deliberately. To see to it that we are not scraping the "bottom of the barrel" when it comes to affection, love, and humility for the people that we love most, we should ask God to fill us up beyond capacity so that we do not give others, including our children, something that we do not have enough of.

When we give from our portion of what is vital for our own survival and growth, we soon begin to live a life of resentment and possible regret. We give all that we are and when our children grow up and leave the nest, we are left an empty shell, deeply searching for meaning and contentment. On the contrary, when we give to our precious babies out of our overflow, we are filling them with potential, goals, dreams, love, discipline, respect, resilience all while being filled ourselves. The residual blessing that comes from this produces deep fulfillment and purpose.

As we continue this life driven by intentional prayer, we find that our faith develops a muscle that won't allow us to grow faint in our pursuit of being good parents. After we have been filled and we teach and train our children from this healthy state, we will begin to see the fruit of all our labor, and we will remain full.

Recite this prayer:

Dear Heavenly Father,

Help me to be intentional with my prayers. Teach me to pray specific prayers according to my need and desire. I long to spend more time with you. Help me to not rush our time we get to spend together. My desire is to operate out of my overflow and I understand, in Your presence, I am filled.

In Jesus name, Amen.

SPILL YOUR HEART

DAY 28

INTENTIONAL PRAYER

1 Thessalonians 5:16-18 says, "Rejoice always, pray continually, give thanks in all circumstances; for this is God's will for you in Christ Jesus." I know sometimes it seems like we don't possess the strength to praise God in certain circumstances in our lives, however, allow me to submit to you that praise in the form of prayer is the best way to regain strength in our weakness. We gain power and authority through humility when we muster up the strength to give thanks when life feels like it is falling apart. To utter the words "thank you" to the Father when it seems insane to rejoice, magnifies our God, gives us power, moves what was standing in the way out of the way, and gives us access to Heavenly resources for our situations. The message we are conveying to our obstacles and the darkness behind them is that our focus is not on the fear that

is taunting us, our focus will remain on God. Our battles belong to God and the victory belongs to us!

Our enemy, the devil, is as big as we make him, and we should choose, at all cost, to resist him completely! We can learn a great deal from Job; a righteous man who walked upright before the Lord and embodied integrity. The enemy attacked him on every end. He lost his wealth, his health, even his entire family but he refused to turn away from God! His faith was proven by the way he chose to bless the Lord even in the midst of losing not some, but all of his children! Job's prayer life was evident when he said in Job 13:15, "Though He slays me, yet will I hope in Him."

We can only hope to have the strength that Job had, but hope is our reality! When you are challenged today, or when the crumb snatchers get on your nerves, let's let our first words be, "Thank you Lord." It gives you access to so much power and allows you to maintain control of your obstacles.

Recite this Prayer:

Dear Heavenly Father,

What an example You have given us in Your servant Job! I pray for even a quarter of the faith Job exercised in his life through his prayers. I choose to rejoice always with the strength that only You can provide.

In Jesus name, Amen.

SPILL YOUR HEART

_____

_____

_____

_____

_____

_____

_____

_____

_____

_____

_____

_____

_____

_____

_____

_____

_____

_____

DAY 29

INTENTIONAL PRAYER

Sometimes, life can deal rather harsh blows. The pain of hardships can feel unbearable at times. Prayer is the key that unlocks the peace God gives. Prayer is how we get Heaven's attention here on earth. Jesus said that our Father in Heaven knows what we need before we even ask Him (Matthew 6:8). He gave us clear instruction on how we should pray.

Matthew 6:9-10 says, "Pray like this: Our Father in Heaven, may Your name be kept Holy. May Your Kingdom come soon. May Your will be done on earth, as it is in Heaven." It is in this text that we discover that prayer is the way we relinquish Heaven's resources onto the earth. 2 Corinthians 10:4 says, "The weapons we fight with are not the weapons of the world. On the contrary, they have divine power to demolish strongholds." Prayer is also the most powerful secret weapon we possess as believers, that break strongholds or strong un-Godly habits or generational cycles...things that are hard to get rid of. If we understand the true power of prayer, it would no longer be our last resort, but something we would automatically carve intentional time out of our busy lives to do.

What if I told you that prayer accompanied with faith can operate faster than first responders?! Prayers can even bring about lasting healing that not even the best doctors possess the power nor the education to administer. Take this week to carve out intentional time to pray and watch your life change drastically.

Recite this Prayer:

Dear Heavenly Father,

Strengthen my prayer life. Give me the desire to call upon You for every little detail of my life. I desire to know You more and trust You more. I admit that I can do nothing on my own. I need You and Your resources to carry me through this journey called life.

In Jesus name, Amen.

SPILL YOUR HEART

DAY 30

INTENTIONAL PRAYER

What I love most about our, living, God is that He is not like a statue that remains mute when we are desiring to communicate with Him. Our prayers do not fall on deaf ears because He is always available whenever we call on Him. In fact, there are several moments in scripture that shed light on our living and breathing God who desires to communicate with us by answering our prayers.

1 Chronicles 4:10 says, " Jabez cried out to the God of Israel, "Oh, that You would bless me and enlarge my territory! Let Your hand be with me and keep me from harm so that I will be free from pain." And God granted his request." Another favorite example in scripture is when God shows His involvement in prayer. 2 Chronicles 7:14 says, "If my people, who are called by my name, will humble themselves and pray and seek my face and turn from their wicked ways, then I will hear from Heaven, and I

will forgive their sin and will heal their land." David said in Psalm 86:6-8, "Hear my prayer, Lord; listen to my cry for mercy. When I am in distress, I call to you, because you answer me. Among the gods there is none like you, Lord; no deeds can compare with Yours."

Let these answered prayers give you the fuel you need to get into the presence of your ever breathing, always listening God who is eagerly anticipating your request to show you His matchless and marvelous wonders. I leave you with the peace that is found in Philippians 4:6-7 that says, "Do not be anxious about anything, but in every situation, by prayer and petition, with thanksgiving, present your requests to God. And the peace of God, which transcends all understanding, will guard your hearts and your minds in Christ Jesus."

Recite this Prayer:

Lord,

Thank you for Your willingness to not only answer my prayers but Your eagerness to simply hear my voice. Forgive me for allowing the smallest things to distract me from getting into Your presence. Now that I've experienced Your presence, it's where I aspire to remain. God even when You don't answer my prayers the way I would like, I know and trust that whatever You do is going to work out in my favor. Thank You!

In Jesus name I pray, Amen.

SPILL YOUR HEART

Thank You

It is with great love and motivation that I spilled my heart on each of these pages with the great hope that they will speak life into the dark, depleted and breathless areas of your life.

It is my goal to SHOCK your heart back to a state of gratitude, hope, and direction while infusing inspiration with each word that I've not just written but live out daily. "Therefore, since we are surrounded by such a huge crowd of witnesses to the life of faith, let us strip off every weight that slows us down, especially the sin that so easily trips us up. And let us run with endurance the race God has set before us. We do this by keeping our eyes on Jesus, the champion who initiates and perfects our faith. Because of the joy awaiting Him, He endured the cross, disregarding its shame. Now, He is seated in the place of honor beside God's throne." ~Hebrews 12:1-2

NOW GO KISS ALL OVER THOSE

CHILDREN OF YOURS AND TELL

THEM HOW MUCH YOU LOVE

THEM!!!!

Made in the USA
Columbia, SC
21 April 2019